BLACK

AND

WHITE

FROM

A TO Z

BY: MATT WEBER

ILLUSTRATED BY: AN ANT

ISBN-13: 978-1-949356-01-4

FOR MY DAD, Jeff Weber

BLACK from A to Z

ASPHALT

BOWLING BALL

COAL

DARTH VADER

EIGHT BALL

FLAG

GARBAGE BAG

HOLE

INK

JAMAICAN FLAG

KNIGHT

LIMOUSINE

MAMBA

NINJA

OLIVE

PANTHER

QUOTATION MARK

RAVEN

SHARPIE

TIRE

UMPIRE

VULTURE

WITCH

X-RAY

YEMEN FLAG

ZORRO

WHITE from A to Z

AVALANCHE

BASEBALL

CUE BALL

DISH

EGG

FLOUR

GLUE

HORCHATA

IGLOO

JICAMA

KLEENEX

LIGHT BULB

MARSHMALLOW

NURSE

ONION

POLAR BEAR

QUILTED NORTHERN

RICE

SALT

TALC

UNICORN

VANILLA

WEDDING
DRESS

X-MAS
STAR

YARROW

ZURICH

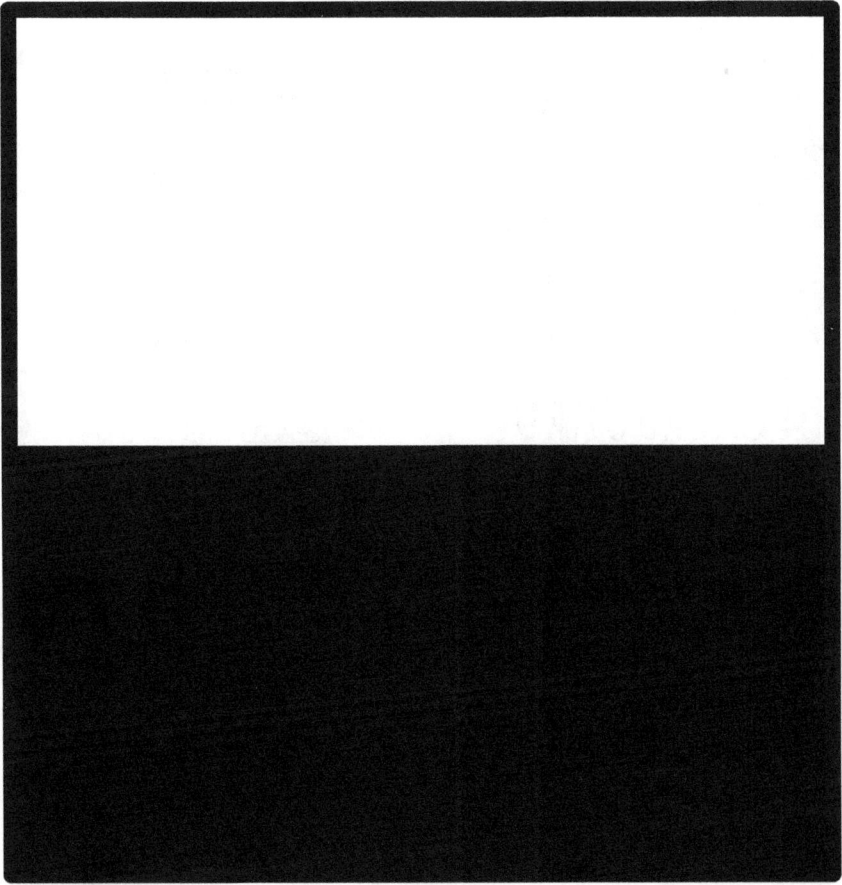

BLACK AND WHITE FROM A TO Z

ACE OF SPADES

BUTLER

CHECKERBOARD

DALMATIAN

EYEBALL

FOOTBALL

GUINNESS

HABIT

INDRI

JOLLY ROGER

KILLER WHALE

LEMUR TAIL

MAGPIE

NEWSPAPER

OREO

PIANO

QR CODE

REFEREE

SNOOPY

TUXEDO

UNDERLINE

VAMPIRE

WHITE SOX

XYLOPHONE

YIN & YANG

ZEBRA

FROM A TO Z

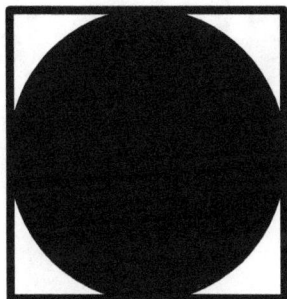

APERTURE

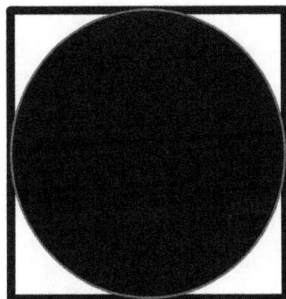

BASS CLEF

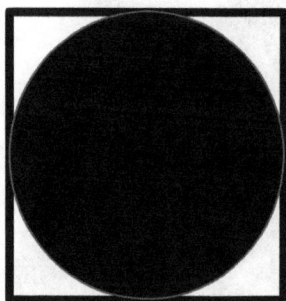

COLON

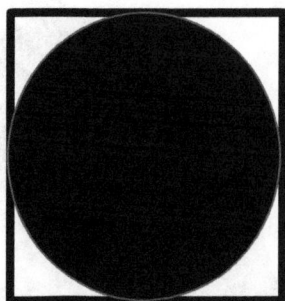

DOMINO

ELLIPSIS

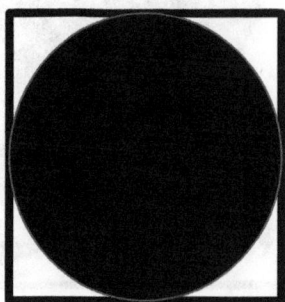

FUNGUS

GOOGLY EYE

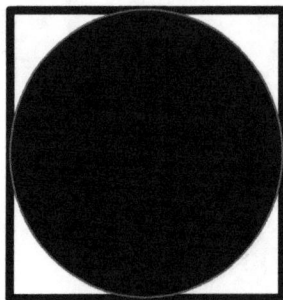

HOLE PUNCHED

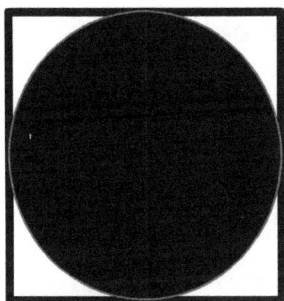

INK SPOT

JAGUAR

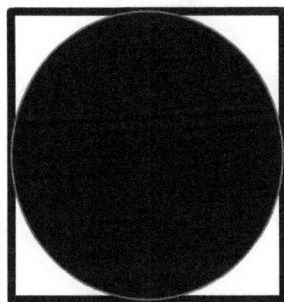

KIWI SEED

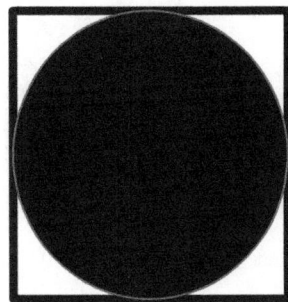

LINE PLOT

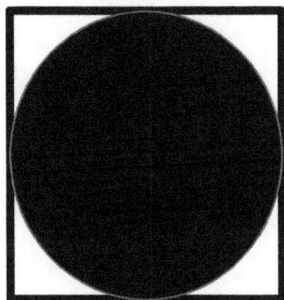

MOLE

NEGATIVE SPACE

OIL DROP

POLKADOT

QUESTION MARK

RABBIT DROPPING

SNAKE EYES

TATTOO START

UNICODE
FULL STOP

VINYL

WORMHOLE

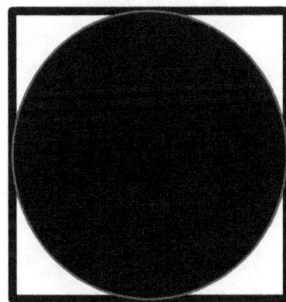

EXCLAMATION
POINT

YAHTZEE

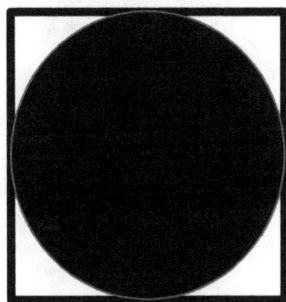

ZEBRA PUPIL

GRAY FROM A TO Z

ASHES

BATTLESHIP

CEMENT

DUMBBELL

ELEPHANT

FOG

GAMEBOY

HINDENBURG

IRON

JACKRABBIT

KOALA

LINT

MANTA RAY

NICKEL

OSTRICH

PEWTER

QUARTZITE

RHINO

SMOKE

TORNADO

U-BOAT

VOLCANIC ASH

WHALE

XEME

YUCATAN SQUIRREL

ZINC

THE
END

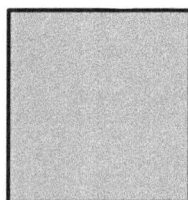

www.ingramcontent.com/pod-product-compliance
Lightning Source LLC
Chambersburg PA
CBHW071804020426
42331CB00008B/2398